D1538294

EDGE BOOKS™

Prepare to Survive

How to Survive an
EARTHQUAKE

by Heather Montgomery

Consultant: Al Siebert, PhD
Author of *The Survivor Personality*

Capstone press®

Mankato, Minnesota

Edge Books are published by Capstone Press,
151 Good Counsel Drive, P.O. Box 669, Mankato, Minnesota 56002.
www.capstonepress.com

Library of Congress Cataloging-in-Publication Data
Montgomery, Heather.
How to survive an earthquake / by Heather Montgomery.
p. cm. — (Edge books. Prepare to survive)
Summary: "Briefly presents specific survival strategies that can be used in
various earthquake survival situations" — Provided by publisher.
Includes bibliographical references and index.
ISBN-13: 978-1-4296-2279-0 (hardcover)
ISBN-10: 1-4296-2279-2 (hardcover)
1. Earthquakes — Juvenile literature. 2. Emergency management — Juvenile
literature. I. Title.
QE521.3.M637 2009
613.6'9 — dc22   2008030623

Editorial Credits
Carrie A. Braulick, editor; Veronica Bianchini, designer; Wanda Winch,
    photo researcher; Sarah L. Schuette, photo stylist; Marcy Morin,
    photo shoot scheduler

Photo Credits
AP Images/Mark J. Terrill, 9 (landslide); AP Images/Michael Mariant, cover;
Capstone Press/Karon Dubke, 12 (pillow), 12–13, 13 (lower right), 14 (both), 20,
21, 24 (both), 26 (both), 28, 29; City of Santa Ana Public Library, Local History
Room, 25; FEMA News Photo, 15; Getty Images Inc./AFP/AFP, 22; Getty
Images Inc./AFP/Asahi Shimbun, 10; Getty Images Inc./AFP/Pierre Verdy, 9
(leaning building); Getty Images Inc./China Photos, 18; Newscom/AFP, 27; Peter
Arnold/Altitude, 4–5; Peter Arnold/Wilco van Herpen, 17; Rod Whigham, 11, 16,
19, 23; Shutterstock/Lora Liu, back cover (grunge notebook)

The author would like to acknowledge Larry Collins, captain of the California
Urban Search and Rescue Task Force, for sharing his expertise and reviewing this
manuscript. She would also like to thank her brother for his research assistance
and her husband for his endless support.

1 2 3 4 5 6 14 13 12 11 10 09

Table of Contents

Chapter 1

SHAKING BENEATH YOUR FEET

You're sound asleep in bed. Suddenly, your bed shakes. DVDs tumble onto the floor. Glasses rattle in the kitchen. Earthquake!

You might think that earthquakes can't happen where you live. After all, they are common only in Alaska, California, Hawaii, and a few other states. Yet earthquakes can happen anywhere. They can be so powerful that they bring down buildings or so mild that no one even notices them. Several hundred earthquakes occur across the planet every day.

An earthquake can happen at any time. One could make you miss your basketball shot. One could shake you awake in the middle of the night. Will you be ready?

TIP: Want to avoid earthquakes? Move to a state with few earthquakes. These states include Florida, Iowa, North Dakota, and Delaware.

An earthquake is simply the shaking of the ground. The earth's crust, or top layer, is broken into large masses called **plates**. If the plates slip quickly past one another, an earthquake occurs.

The earth's plates constantly move. We don't notice the movement because the plates move only about as fast as our fingernails grow.

Normally, the plates move smoothly. Imagine sliding together the soles of two dress shoes. The smooth soles would slide easily.

Now imagine sliding together the soles of running shoes. The traction on their soles would catch and stick. That's what can happen to plates. When the smooth motion between the plates stops, the earth continues trying to move. Tension builds at the sticking point. After the tension becomes great enough, the edges give way. The plates slip swiftly to a new position, causing an earthquake.

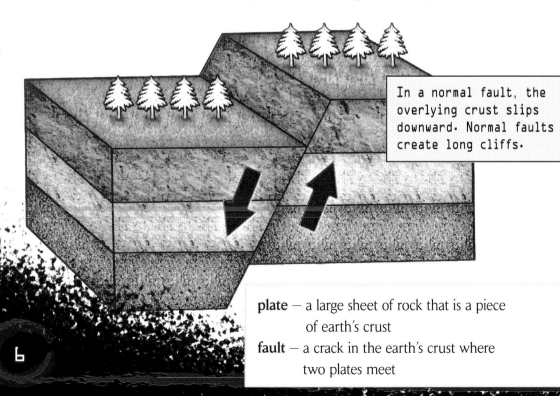

In a normal fault, the overlying crust slips downward. Normal faults create long cliffs.

plate — a large sheet of rock that is a piece of earth's crust
fault — a crack in the earth's crust where two plates meet

Most earthquakes happen along cracks in the earth's crust. The cracks are called **faults**. Two plates meet at a fault. The plate edges are more likely to catch and stick together there.

MODIFIED MERCALLI INTENSITY SCALE

I.	Usually not felt.
II.	Felt only by a few people who are either at rest or on the upper floors of buildings.
III.	Many people indoors feel movement, especially if they are on the upper floors of buildings.
IV.	Most people indoors feel movement. Hanging objects swing. Dishes, windows, and doors rattle. Parked vehicles rock.
V.	Felt by nearly everyone. Sleeping people are awakened. Some dishes and windows break. Unstable objects overturn.
VI.	Some heavy furniture moves. Wall plaster may crack and fall. Damage is slight.
VII.	Damage is slight to moderate in well-constructed buildings. Damage is considerable in poorly constructed buildings. Some chimneys break.
VIII.	Damage is slight in reinforced buildings. Considerable damage occurs in buildings that are not reinforced. Poorly built structures suffer severe damage. Chimneys and towers fall. Heavy furniture overturns.
IX.	Damage is considerable in reinforced buildings. Buildings move off their foundations. Well-constructed buildings suffer great damage, sometimes with partial collapse.
X.	Some well-built wooden structures are destroyed. Most masonry and frame buildings and their foundations are destroyed. Some railroad tracks bend.
XI.	Few, if any, masonry structures remain standing. Bridges are destroyed. Railroad tracks bend considerably.
XII.	Damage is nearly total or total. Objects are thrown into the air. Large amounts of rock may move.

The Modified Mercalli Intensity Scale uses Roman numerals to measure an earthquake's effects.

EARTHQUAKE DANGERS

Earthquakes can create dangers that are just as unpredictable as the earthquakes themselves. As you might guess, windows may shatter and books might fly off shelves. But that's not all. Earthquakes can cause fires, floods, landslides, and many other dangers.

BUCKLING BUILDINGS

Movies show huge cracks in the earth as the most dangerous part of an earthquake. Although these cracks can happen, the real danger is caused by the shaking ground. The shaking earth can throw a building off its foundation or cause a building to collapse. People can lose their homes or have their belongings crushed. Worst of all, they may be trapped underneath a collapsed building's **rubble**.

rubble — broken bricks and stone left after a building has collapsed

FLAMES AND FRENZY

In places where earthquakes are common, buildings are **reinforced**. They are anchored to their foundations. Some buildings are built on top of rubber springs to absorb the shock of an earthquake.

Yet even if you are in a reinforced building, gas lines can leak and damaged electrical wires can create sparks. These occurrences can start a fire or cause an explosion. If the water pipes are also broken, no water can get to the fire hydrants. Things can get pretty nasty.

A fire broke out after an earthquake in Kobe, Japan, on January 17, 1995.

reinforced – strengthened

Tsunamis slow down and get larger as they near the coast.

FLOODS AND LANDSLIDES

Flooding is another danger. An earthquake on the ocean floor can send waves that are 50 to 100 feet (15 to 30 meters) tall onto shore. These waves are called tsunamis. A tsunami can flood a city in minutes.

You have to watch out for landslides too. When the ground shakes, dirt acts like a liquid. It flows downhill, covering everything in its path.

By now, earthquakes probably sound like your worst nightmare. But using the survival tips on the following pages will help keep you safe.

Chapter 2

HOW TO SURVIVE

TIP: If you have a pillow nearby, use it to protect your head from falling objects.

Staying calm is one of the best things you can do in an earthquake. If you panic, you won't be able to think clearly. You might mistake the sounds of a landslide for the passing of a nearby train. Or you might not notice the best place to take cover.

IF YOU'RE IN A STURDY BUILDING

If you're in a reinforced or other sturdy building during an earthquake, drop to the floor. Next, find cover. At this point, your worst enemy will be your own stuff. Picture frames may fly off the wall. Stereo speakers could tumble onto your head. Crawl under a desk, table, or another piece of sturdy furniture. Hold on to the furniture to keep it from sliding across the floor.

If there is no sturdy furniture for cover, crouch or sit against an interior wall away from windows. Make sure there is no tall furniture nearby that could fall on you. Cover your head with your hands.

What if

YOU'RE IN AN OLD BUILDING?

If the building you're in was built before 1978, you need a different survival plan. Older buildings are more likely to collapse. Old brick and **adobe** buildings are the most risky. Crouch between two sturdy pieces of furniture like a bed and a heavy desk. If the ceiling caves in, you'll be better protected.

What if

YOU'RE IN BED?

If you're in bed, stay there. Pull the blankets over your body and put a pillow over your head. Even if the bed starts sliding, stay there. It is safer than trying to move when everything around you is shifting.

If staying in bed does become unsafe, roll out of the bed. Lie on the floor right next to your bed. The bed could shield you from falling debris.

adobe — a brick made of clay and straw that is dried in the sun

NOT JUST ANOTHER EARTHQUAKE

Twelve-year-old Hayes Stuppy was used to earthquakes. They happened often in his hometown of Northridge, California. When the walls shook on the night of January 17, 1994, Hayes didn't worry. He lay in bed instead of moving. Then the roaring sound got louder. Bang! His bookcase hit the floor. Falling objects missed Hayes because he had stayed in bed.

Hayes then realized the earthquake was bigger than he had first thought. After the shaking stopped, he ran out of his room. Hayes found his family downstairs — everyone except his father.

Hayes found his father in the upstairs bathroom. A gash ran up his dad's left ankle. A pool of blood covered the floor. Within seconds, Hayes' father became unconscious. Hayes then thought of his Boy Scout training. He used first aid to stop the bleeding. Hayes' dad then awoke and was taken to the hospital.

Although Hayes later said he was just being lazy, staying in bed probably helped save his life. Hayes' 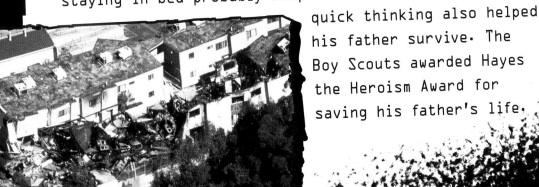 quick thinking also helped his father survive. The Boy Scouts awarded Hayes the Heroism Award for saving his father's life.

What if

YOU'RE TRAPPED IN RUBBLE?

If a building collapses on you, cover your mouth and nose with your shirt or a cloth. Some people die from breathing in too much dust. If you can, grab a dust mask, a flashlight, and a whistle or cell phone.

Stay calm. Don't shout for help — you'll breathe in dust. Shouting will also tire you. Instead, use a whistle or a cell phone to notify rescue workers that you need help. You can also knock on a pipe or wall with something hard, like a piece of concrete or metal. Tap three times, pause, and tap again. Rescue workers will be listening for that pattern.

Dehydration is one of the biggest threats when you are trapped. **Conserve** the water that is already inside your body by breathing through your nose instead of your mouth. If you are hot, take off extra layers of clothing and slowly fan yourself.

If you have water, drink only when you are thirsty. When you run out of water, you might be tempted to drink your urine. Gross, right? People have done it before. But you shouldn't. That will dehydrate you even more.

dehydration — a medical condition caused by a lack of water
conserve — to save

TRAPPED!

On August 17, 1999, an earthquake struck 13-year-old Onur Ümit's hometown of Gölcük, Turkey. His family's apartment building crashed down around him. Then everything went silent.

Surprisingly, Onur was not seriously hurt. But he was trapped. He had only 11 inches (28 centimeters) between what had been his room's ceiling and the floor. Onur couldn't even turn his head. But Onur had watched a TV show on survival, so he knew what to do. He didn't waste his energy yelling. Instead, he broke a leg off a chair and banged the chair leg against the wall.

Then Onur waited. He tried to stay calm and be still to save his energy. He repeated a comedy skit in his head to keep up his spirits.

Above Onur, rescue workers and Onur's family searched through the ruins. Five floors of concrete lay between them and Onur. After 18 hours, Onur heard someone call his name. Onur called back. Rescue workers dug furiously until they reached him. After 27 hours, Onur escaped from the building that could have become his grave.

Rescuers worked tirelessly to find survivors after the earthquake that hit Gölcük, Turkey, in 1999.

What if

THE BRIDGE BREAKS?

During an earthquake, bridges can collapse. If your car plunges into the water, the water pressure will make it too hard to open the door. Try to stay calm. A car will usually float for 45 seconds. Do everything possible to open and crawl out a side window before the car sinks. Try pushing on the corner of the window with a strong pointed object such as a key. You can also try kicking out the window.

A strong earthquake struck China in 2008, causing the Xiaoyudong Bridge to collapse.

If the car sinks before you can get out, wait until the water level in your car is about halfway up the side window. At that point, the water pressure on the inside and outside of the car should be almost equal. Take a breath of air and open a window or a door. Be prepared for a small rush of water. Then swim to the surface.

TIP: Keep a construction tool called a center punch or another sharp object in your car. You can use it to easily break a side window in an emergency.

How to

SURVIVE A FIRE

Damaged gas lines and electrical cords can start fires after an earthquake. Most small fires can be put out with a fire extinguisher, water, or dirt. But if the fire appears to be electrical, don't use water. The electrical current could travel through the water and shock you. Instead, turn off the electricity at the breaker box. The breaker box is probably in your basement, a closet, or the garage. Then smother the fire with baking soda or use a Class C fire extinguisher.

If you're in a burning building, don't waste time trying to save your stuff. Crawl along the floor toward an outside exit. There is less smoke at lower heights. If you come to a closed door, check if it is hot before you open it. If it is hot, there is a fire on the other side. Find another way out. If the room is very smoky, breathe through a piece of wet cloth to protect your lungs. You can use spit to wet the cloth. When you get outside, go far away from the building.

How to

USE A FIRE EXTINGUISHER

1. Pull the pin.
2. Aim the extinguisher nozzle at the base of the flames.
3. Squeeze the trigger.
4. Sweep the extinguisher from side to side until the fire is out.

TIP: Don't light a match or a lighter after an earthquake. If gas lines are leaking nearby, an explosion can occur.

How to

SURVIVE A TSUNAMI

Everyone loves a day at the beach. But if you're on an ocean beach after an earthquake, a tsunami could have you running for your life. Move to higher ground if you feel an earthquake. If the water at the shore rises or falls suddenly, that's a big warning sign. Run to a tall building. Try to get 100 feet (30 meters) above the shoreline. That height is higher than a three-story building.

If you can't get inside a building, climb a tree. If you're swept away, try to grab onto something that floats.

Water drawing back near the coast is a warning that a tsunami is coming. Run as fast as you can to higher ground.

How to

SURVIVE A LANDSLIDE

If you hear rumbling or tree branches snapping after an earthquake, you could be in a landslide's path. Get inside a sturdy building — one that withstood the earthquake should do. Go to the highest story. Find the room that is farthest from the slide. Then crawl under a sturdy desk or table.

If you can't make it inside, run away from the landslide at an angle. If the landslide catches you, curl up into a ball and protect your head with your arms. As you fall, yell for help so rescuers will know where to find you.

What If

SPILLED CHEMICALS ARE NEARBY?

Bet you didn't know that kitty litter can save your life! During an earthquake, household cleaners and other chemicals often spill. They could burn your skin if you touch them. They could also mix and cause an explosion. Use kitty litter to soak up chemicals before that happens.

If you don't have kitty litter, get your feet off the floor. Make a bridge with furniture, boxes, or stacks of books. Walk or climb over the spilled chemicals to safety.

TIP: Keep comfortable shoes by your bed. They will protect your feet from glass and other debris after an earthquake.

GOOD THINKING!

An earthquake on March 10, 1933, in Long Beach, California, trapped a man in his paint store. He wasn't trapped by a collapsed building, though. He couldn't leave because spilled paint and other liquids with chemicals swirled across the floor. He knew that mixed chemicals can be dangerous. He turned two empty paint cans upside down and tied them to his boots. Then he stomped right out of the store.

The 1933 earthquake that struck Long Beach, California, damaged several buildings, including this school.

What if

YOU'RE STRANDED?

If you've survived a really big earthquake, your troubles could last for a while. The roads may be unusable. You may be stuck without household water, gas, or electricity.

In this situation, having enough drinking water will be most important. Germs may have infected the water supply. Don't drink tap water unless local officials have announced that it is safe. Drink bottled water instead. If you must drink tap water, pour it through a coffee filter or paper towel to strain out dirt. Then add eight drops of bleach to every gallon of water. You can also use water purification tablets.

If you aren't able to cook, eat canned and dried foods. Fresh and frozen foods spoil quickly if they aren't kept cold.

In the days and weeks after an earthquake, be prepared for more shaking beneath your feet. **Aftershocks** can destroy buildings that are already damaged.

Relief workers may supply drinking water after an earthquake. But knowing how to purify water will keep you healthy until relief supplies arrive.

TIP: Plan an emergency meeting place with your family. This will help you find one another if you become separated after a disaster.

aftershock – a small earthquake that follows a larger one

MAKE A SURVIVAL KIT

A survival kit will help you stay safe after an earthquake. Include the following items:

- first-aid kit
- 1 gallon (3.8 liters) of bottled water per person, per day
- dried or canned food
- nonelectric can opener
- glow sticks
- dust masks
- flashlights with extra batteries
- battery-powered radio

- whistle
- comfortable shoes
- gas shut-off wrench
- bleach
- extra clothing
- water purification tablets
- pet food, if you have pets

BE PREPARED!

You have just learned several ways to survive if you are caught off guard by an earthquake. But surviving is easier if you are prepared. Secure small objects on shelves with putty. Ask an adult to help you secure bookcases and other furniture that is taller than it is wide. Look around your school and other places where you spend a lot of time. Find the best places to take cover.

Earthquakes are powerful acts of nature. They shake up our world and create many dangers. You can't predict or stop earthquakes, but being prepared will help you stay safe.

Glossary

adobe (uh-DOH-bee) — a brick made of clay and straw that is dried in the sun

aftershock (AF-tur-shok) — a small earthquake that follows a larger one

conserve (kuhn-SURV) — to save

current (KUHR-uhnt) — the movement of electricity through a wire or other conductor

dehydration (dee-hy-DRAY-shuhn) — a life-threatening medical condition caused by a lack of water

fault (FAWLT) — a crack in the earth where two plates meet; earthquakes often occur along faults.

foundation (foun-DAY-shuhn) — a solid structure on which a building is built

plate (PLAYT) — a large sheet of rock that is a piece of earth's crust

putty (PUHT-ee) — a type of soft cement made of powdered chalk and linseed oil; putty becomes hard when it dries.

reinforced (ree-in-FORSSED) — strengthened to withstand an earthquake

rubble (RUHB-uhl) — broken bricks and stones

tsunami (tsoo-NAH-mee) — a large, destructive wave created by an underwater earthquake

Read More

Krohn, Katherine. *The Earth-Shaking Facts About Earthquakes with Max Axiom, Super Scientist.* Graphic Science. Mankato, Minn.: Capstone Press, 2008.

Roza, Greg. *Earthquake: True Stories of Survival.* Survivor Stories. New York: Rosen Central, 2007.

Walker, Sally M. *Earthquakes.* Early Bird Earth Science. Minneapolis: Lerner, 2008.

Internet Sites

FactHound offers a safe, fun way to find educator-approved Internet sites related to this book.

Here's what you do:

1. Visit *www.facthound.com*
2. Choose your grade level.
3. Begin your search.

This book's ID number is 9781429622790.

FactHound will fetch the best sites for you!

Index